Communication Strategies for Adult Children Supporting Aging Parents at Home

By Christina Newberry

COMMUNICATION STRATEGIES FOR ADULT CHILDREN
SUPPORTING AGING PARENTS AT HOME

ISBN 978-0-9813900-4-8

Table of Contents

Introduction

No matter why your parent is living in your home, the good news is that you can make it work.

Whether it's financial troubles or challenges due to aging that have caused your parent to move into your home, the simple truth is that you are not alone.

A recent survey by the National Alliance for Caregiving and the American Association of Retired Persons showed that nearly a quarter of U.S. households — an estimated 22.4 million — are caring for someone 50 or older, or have provided that care during the previous 12 months. According to the Pew Research Center, 30 percent of adult children in the United States contribute financially to their parents' care. And 3.6 million elderly parents have moved into their adult children's homes full time.

ICON KEY

✏ **Assignment**

☝ **Helpful Tip**

It hasn't always been this way. The number of elderly parents living with adult children has increased by 67% in the last 9 years, according to U.S. Census data.

So what's causing all these multi-generational households? One possible cause is the skyrocketing cost of assisted living – and the accompanying fact that many seniors' retirement funds have taken a beating.

In some cases it's actually a mutually beneficial plan financially, since the adult children may be struggling to afford their own home payments in a challenging economy. Plus, both parents and adult children may crave the emotional support an extra adult in the home can offer.

No matter why your parent has moved into your home, you can make it work. But you'll need to do some planning – and a lot of talking – to make sure it works out for the best for everyone.

In this book you'll discover some key strategies to keeping everyone in your household happy – even with an extra adult around. The most important thing is to make sure you have good, solid, open communication, and we'll talk a lot about that in this book.

Topic 1:
Why Communication Is So Important

The most important part of any adult relationship is solid, open communication. Paired with clear expectations, communication is the most important tool you have to ensure your relationship with your parent stays healthy while they're living in your home.

What do we mean by expectations?

Well, the simple truth is that many parents who move in with their children are used to being very independent, and their expectations for independence may not match up with what you think is appropriate given the state of their health or finances. Or, your parent may slip back into the parenting role, and offer you more "helpful advice" than you can stomach.

You must communicate your own needs and expectations right from the beginning.

Helpful Tip: Finances

Have the conversation about expected financial contributions and behaviors before your parent moves in, if possible. If they've already moved in, this is a conversation you need to have as soon as you finish reading this book. You'll get some strategies in later chapters that will make the process much easier, and you can use your bonus Family Meeting Agenda (found at the end of the book) to guide the discussion.

Even if you've always had a great relationship with your parent, it's important to establish the expectations for how they will fit into the day-to-day routine in your home. In addition to the topics covered in the Family Meeting Agenda, here are some tough topics you should discuss with your parent one-on-one:

- **What is their real financial situation?** You need the nitty-gritty details here, as you need to know what options are available to you in terms of caring for your parent, and moving to a care facility if you become unable to manage their care at home. Does your parent have a list of assets? What about debts? Are they receiving a pension, social security, or income from investments?

- **What is their insurance coverage?** Does your parent have medical coverage? What about a prescription plan and long-term care insurance? Life insurance? Make sure you know the names of the providers and understand the coverage. You may want to discuss taking out additional coverage or looking into Medicare and Medicaid.

- **Do they want a living will or power of attorney?** A power of attorney allows the designated person (you) to make decisions about finances on your parent's behalf, even after they are unable to state their own wishes. You cannot take financial action on your parent's behalf without one. A power of attorney for health care (sometimes called a health care proxy) allows the designated person to make decisions about health care on your parent's behalf, in case they are unable to do so when the time comes. A living will allows your parent to state their future wishes if life support is needed. You can create a power of attorney or a living will without hiring a lawyer by using the online resources at *Parting Wishes* (find them online at http://www.christinanewberry.com/partingwishes).

- **What is their real state of health?** Parents often try to shield their adult children about health problems, but you need to know the whole truth when your parent moves in. Ask about medications and recent doctor's visits, and get your parent's doctor's contact information.

When your parent moves in, the expectations need to be clear so that everyone knows what they can expect and what they are responsible for, and so that there can be clear methods of addressing challenges when expectations are not met.

If everyone has the same expectations, you've set yourself up for a much healthier – and easier to manage – situation.

Topic 2:
Typical Family Problems That Happen When Parents Move in with Their Adult Children

And How to Deal With Them!

When two generations of adults live in one household, it's extremely easy for anger, resentment, and guilt to build up on both sides. And once those bitter emotions have crept into a relationship, they are extremely difficult to overcome.

Areas you're most likely to struggle with may include:

- Stress in your relationship with your spouse or partner

- Disagreements over how to parent (or grandparent) your children

---

- Expectations for financial contributions
- Loss of freedom (for your parent *and* for you)

Stress in your relationship with your partner

Having extra people in your house puts a strain on the other relationships you have in your life – especially the relationship you have with your partner.

Of course you want to do the best you can for your parent, but doing so at the expense of your own happiness does *not* make you a better daughter or son.

The best way to overcome the extra challenges placed on your relationship with your partner is to talk to each other about how you're feeling.

Make sure your partner knows how much you value him or her. Your partner has likely never lived with your parent before, and may not have a good existing relationship to build on.

They may suddenly feel a bit like a stranger in their own home, as the partnership they've formed with you is no longer the only adult relationship in the home.

They may even be worried that your relationship with your parent will push your partner to the fringes of your life.

Again, as we'll say over and over again in this book, **open communication is the best strategy.** Tell your partner how much they mean to you, and how much you appreciate the flexibility and caring they are showing by welcoming your parent into the home you share.

And make time – dedicated time – for one another. Plan for dinners away from your parent, so the two of you can continue to have a relationship that is really focused on what the two of you enjoy about one another.

Disagreements over how to parent (or grandparent) your children

When a grandparent moves into a household that still has young children living in it, there can be conflict between the parents and the grandparent over how to raise the children.

Grandparents are used to being able to spoil their grandchildren, but the relationship and expectations have to change when the grandparent is living in the same home. Your parent also needs to understand that when it comes to the kids, you're in charge.

Your children may also have concerns about having a grandparent move in. Adding another person to the household will mean changes to the amount of personal space and privacy they have – and may mean additional responsibilities if the grandparent is unwell.

Teenagers may be prone to bratty behavior in the best of circumstances, and any challenging situation has the potential to put their attitude into overdrive.

The best way to avert the sulking or complaining that may come from your children is, again, communication. Be very clear about why your parent is moving in, and tell your children that everyone is going to make an effort to keep things as normal in the household as possible.

And again, make sure everybody is talking to each other to head off problems *before* they happen!

Expectations for financial contributions

The reality is, an extra person in your home means additional expenses – for food, heat, electricity, and gas. You need to have an open and honest conversation with your parent about who is responsible for what in terms of the family budget.

Assignment: Create a Budget

Create a family budget to determine how best to handle your parent's contribution to the household. Use the template in Appendix 3 to help you. (We'll talk more about the details of building a family budget in the next chapter, but you can easily start the process now and refine it later.)

Loss of freedom (for your parent and for you)

You're used to a certain level of freedom and privacy – especially if you're an empty nester. You may not run naked through the kitchen, but there's something satisfying about knowing you could if you really wanted to.

Your parent, too, will be used to the freedom of living as an independent adult, so they may be smarting at the anticipation of how much freedom they stand to lose.

While the simple truth is that there *will* be a loss of freedom for you and your parent – it's unavoidable when you all live in the same house – the good news is that by establishing some simple guidelines, you can ensure a reasonable degree of freedom and privacy is maintained.

The family meeting template that came with this book is a great tool to help you establish expectations and guidelines to make sure everyone understands exactly how they'll have to compromise in this area – and what is simply unacceptable.

Helpful Tip:
Remember Your Spouse

Remember: When your parent moves in, your life changes dramatically – and your lifestyle, personal space, and intimacy with your spouse may all be dramatically affected.

The person who will feel most awkward and unsettled in this situation is your spouse. We're pretty sure it's not their dream situation to be living with their in-laws, so any steps you can take to make them feel like they are still an important focus in your life will be helpful to everyone.

Topic 3:
House "Rules" When Your Parent Lives in Your Home

Whatever the reasons for their being in your home, you simply can't control your parent's life.

A key step is recognizing the difference between what happens in your house and what happens in your parent's life. You are certainly able to set the guidelines for behavior in your home, but you cannot set the rules for your parent's life, and you cannot try to control what they do when they are not at home.

Having a Family Meeting

It may feel strange to have a "meeting" and set up "rules," but the best way to discuss – and stick to – household guidelines that everyone is comfortable with is to have a family meeting, complete with agenda and someone taking minutes.

You'll find a family meeting agenda you can use to steer your conversation in Appendix 2.

If your parent is bristling a little bit at the idea of having a meeting and putting things in writing, make sure they know that the agreements you'll be making as part of the process establish guidelines for your behavior too.

One of the most important rules for all of you to follow is to stay out of each other's personal space.

No adult should have to worry about someone digging around in their sock drawer.

Building a budget – and sticking to it

Another key part of the house "rules" is establishing who's going to contribute what in terms of household expenses.

The first step is to work out a budget for your household and ensure it's something *everyone* can live with. Take a look at the budget you developed in Chapter 2. Make sure your parent is comfortable with the amount you'll be asking them to contribute.

If you don't know where the money to make the situation work will come from, you need to think long and hard about whether you actually can help your parent by having them live at your home.

The big question: Who's in charge of the TV?

One of the most aggravating areas of conflict in any family can be the ongoing fight over who gets to choose what the family watches on TV. If your parent has a TV in their own room, this may not be an issue. But if you've only got one TV for the household, it can become surprisingly explosive!

You'll need to talk about who gets to be in charge of the remote. If you have certain programs you follow, it's perfectly reasonable that you should expect to continue to watch those shows. Your parent, though, may also have programs that make up part of their daily routine.

Helpful Tip:
Coordinating TV Schedules

If you both have programs you follow that are on at the same time, alternate who gets to watch their show as its airs. See if you can make everyone happy by recording one show on a VCR or TiVo to watch later, or catching up on missed episodes online.

Another common problem revolves around the family telephone. These days, more people have cell phones, but often aging parents rely on the home phone as a communication lifeline. Make sure you and your parent have a clear understanding of how much long distance calls cost, and when the best time is to call to take advantage of the lowest rates. And, most importantly, make sure everyone is diligent about taking messages for one another!

What about the family car? Are you going to give your parent access to the car, or do they have their own? What about added gas and insurance costs?

Assignment:
Have a Family Meeting

All of these issues (and many more) are covered in the family meeting agenda in Appendix 2. Use the agenda to guide your family meeting and establish guidelines for the use of family resources that everyone can live with.

Topic 4:
Communication Strategies to Maintain Peace in Your Household

Communication is critically important in any relationship, whether it's with your spouse, your boss, your kids, or your aging parent. But it can be especially challenging to understand how to effectively communicate with your parents when they're living in your home.

You need an effective communication strategy.

The first thing you should know is that what you say is not nearly as important as how you say it. Studies have shown that the actual words used only contribute to 7% of a person's understanding of a conversation. Tone makes up 38%, and body language makes up a full 55%!

In this chapter we'll look at key ways for you to establish a healthy and fulfilling relationship with your parent in your home using solid communication techniques.

How to improve your relationship with your aging parent (and everyone else in your home) through direct communication

Too often in life, we are afraid to say what we really mean, or never get to the point of what we actually want to say. When two or more generations of adults are living in the same home, it's critically important to be up front and direct with one another.

Assignment: Learn the Healthy Conversation Formula

An easy way to make sure the conversations you're having with the other adults in your home get to the point of what needs to be discussed is to follow this formula:

When you _____, I feel _____

because I _____.

I would like _____ because _____.

What do you think?

You can use this formula for just about any situation, negative or positive. Here are a couple of examples:

> **"When you** <u>refuse to go to the doctor,</u> **I feel** <u>worried</u> **because I** <u>am concerned about your health</u>. **I would like** <u>you to call Dr. Stanley and make an appointment</u> **because** <u>then we'll get some guidance about the best way to deal with your health issues</u>. **What do you think?"**

> **"When you** <u>spend time with the kids</u> **I feel** <u>so happy</u> **because** <u>I think it's so important them to get to know you better</u>. **I would like** <u>you to pick them up from school on Tuesday</u>. **What do you think?"**

> **"When you** <u>insult Dan</u> **I feel** <u>angry</u> **because** <u>he's my husband and I care about him deeply</u>. **I would like** <u>you to be nicer to Dan</u> **because** <u>he's your son-in-law and he has opened this home to you</u>. **What do you think?"**

It's pretty hard to avoid getting to the point when you follow this formula! It can be a good idea to let the other person respond before starting the "I would like" part of the formula, but don't get distracted!

Even if they are defensive, just carry on with the rest of the formula. You'll be surprised how well it works!

Using listening and discussion principles to create harmony and understanding

The most important thing to any participant in a conversation is that what they have to say is heard and acknowledged by the other person.

Here are some key listening principles to make sure you really understand what is being said to you.

- Listen carefully and don't interrupt.

- Ask questions to clarify any points you don't understand.

- Acknowledge what the other person has said by repeating it back to them in your own words.

- Take time to understand what they've said before jumping in with a response.

… and most importantly, don't spend the whole time someone is talking planning what you're going to say next.

You can't effectively listen while thinking about your own next remark!

Communication techniques to use when you're frustrated or fed up

If your needs and expectations aren't being met, you need to have an honest and constructive conversation with your parent.

But if you want the discussion to be useful, rather than dismissed as "just a fight," you'll need to make sure the points you make are reasonable and clear.

Before trying to explain your unhappiness or disappointment, check what you plan to say for the following four points:

1. **Fair:** If you're going to actually accomplish any change with your parent, the comments you make to them need to be fair. That means the behavior or situation you

want them to change needs to be within their control.

2. **Balanced:** If you're asking your parent to change something that's driving you crazy, try to tell them something they've done that you really appreciate as well.

   They'll be much more receptive to change if they don't feel like *everything* they do is wrong.

3. **Specific:** Vague comments are unlikely to result in any real change. Even if it's uncomfortable, you need to tell your parent quite specifically what needs or expectations are not being met, and what they've done that's creating the problem.

   You also need to be specific about how they can make the situation better, and how the change in behavior will result in a better family environment for everyone.

4. **Immediate:** A sure way to cause a blow-out is to wait until you're mad as heck, then unleash a rant about everything your parent's ever done wrong.

   Deal with each situation as it arises so that nothing gets too out of control. It's not fair to scream at someone now for something they did last month.

Helpful Tip:
Describe, don't judge

No matter who you're trying to communicate with, it's important to remember to use words that are descriptive rather than judgmental.

Try to phrase your comments in a way that expresses your own needs rather than just telling the other person what they're doing wrong.

Here are some examples:

With your parent:

> **Instead of:** "You always leave your wet laundry in the washer and it's driving me crazy!"

> **Try:** "It would make it much easier for me to get my laundry done if you would put your laundry in the dryer."

With your partner:

> **Instead of:** "You're sulking too much about Mom moving home."

> **Try:** "It would make me happy if you could help me figure out the best way to make Mom living at home work out."

The absolute *worst* way to deal with needs or expectations that aren't being met is to be negative and destructive. It

---

can be easy to become destructive in the heat of an argument, and you may not even know you're doing it.

But no matter how angry you get, try to avoid:

- **Being judgmental:** "You don't care about this family!"

- **Name-calling:** "You're such a burden!"

- **Accusations:** "You're always rude to Dan!"

- **Sarcasm:** "You're pretty clever, aren't you!"

… and the most important destructive tactic to avoid:

- **Belittling your parent for their age, or for living with you:** "If you were as tough as you think you are, you wouldn't be stuck here with us!"

Throughout all of the discussions, arguments, and battles you have with your parent (or anyone else, for that matter) remember this important guideline: If you can't think of something good that can be accomplished by any "feedback" you may want to offer, it's better to keep your mouth closed.

Conclusion

We've given you the tools and resources to begin the process of communication with your aging parent.

Having a parent move into your home can be a blessing and a curse to any family. On one hand, it's a chance to develop a stronger, adult-to-adult bond between you and your parent, and for your parent to establish a solid relationship with their grandkids. But it can also be fraught with conflict, as old patterns resurface and are replayed.

Of course, every family's situation is different. For some adults, having a parent move into their home is a readjustment, while for others it can be an upheaval. They key to success in either case is communication.

It can seem like a strange new language to be speaking with a family member – agendas, negotiation, and budgets – but being clear and honest is not only a crucial element to helping you feel comfortable with your parent's arrival in your home, it can also help you, your spouse, and your parent thrive under the circumstances.

There will be setbacks, of course, as there are in any relationship that matters. But if you and your parent can be clear about expectations and communicate effectively, the chances that you will both benefit from the experience are vastly improved. It's a much better way to ensure success than by living on assumptions and hope.

It's crucial, however, that you and your partner be clear about your boundaries, and not be driven by feelings of guilt, or a misguided desire to "help." You can only help your parent if you are doing so in a healthy and voluntary way, and not sacrificing your own relationship, financial security, or peace of mind.

We've given you the tools and resources to begin that process of communication with your parent. Best of luck to you and your family as you learn to renegotiate your relationships!

Appendix 1: Resources

AARP (www.aarp.org)

The AARP is a nonprofit organization that works to enhance the quality of life for Americans over the age of 50. You'll find information on health care, travel and leisure, and financial issues for your parents on their site.

Administration on Aging (www.aoa.gov)

This administration is a federal government advocate agency that offers information on housing, medical issues, caregiving, and services for seniors.

ElderWeb (www.elderweb.com)

Elderweb offers online resources dealing with finances, health care, living arrangements, social issues, mental issues, and legal issues for seniors, their families, and their caregivers.

Peace of Mind Calls (www.peaceofmindcalls.com)

With this service, you can hire professional caregivers to call your parent daily while you are out of town, or even just at work. You will receive an e-mail with a summary of the call or an urgent alert if the call is not picked up. It's a great way to give yourself some peace of mind when you can't check in on your parent yourself.

PartingWishes.com
(www.ChristinaNewberry.com/partingwishes)

PartingWishes has a number of great services that you can work through with your parent. You can help them write a will, or create a power of attorney. You can also help them create a living will, which allows your parent to specify their health care wishes in case they are ever unable to communicate. The service is lawyer-approved, and works in Canada, the United States, and the U.K.

Children of Aging Parents Support Group
(http://health.groups.yahoo.com/group/chck_thmpsn/)

This online support group is run by Children of Aging Parents, a nonprofit organization whose mission is to assist America's caregivers of the elderly.

Alzheimers Foundation of America
(http://www.alzfdn.org/index.htm)

If your parent is suffering from Alzheimers disease, this foundation offers helpful resources and respite care grants you should be aware of.

Appendix 2: Family Meeting Agenda

Opening Comments

We seek to maintain a home atmosphere that is comfortable for everyone. This atmosphere needs to be guided by the mutual respect and concern of individual family members for one another.

The agreements we'll reach in this meeting will help us maintain a sense of order and comfort for all of us.

Topic #1: Living expenses

❑ Talk about the budget you developed using the Family Budget Template in Appendix 3. If you have not completed the family budget, do so now.

❑ Make sure everyone agrees that the numbers in the family budget are reasonable.

❑ Determine how much the parent will contribute to the household finances.

Topic #2: What needs to get done around the house

❑ Talk about cleaning – agree that you and your parent may not have the same standards. If your standards are not up to your parent's, they are welcome to clean but not to nag.

❑ Talk about who will do laundry.

❑ Talk about who will do the cooking.

❑ Talk about who will provide pet care, especially if your parent is bringing a new pet into the home.

❑ Talk about child care, if your parent will be looking after your kids.

Topic #3: Household "Rules"

❑ Talk about any behavior that is unacceptable to you or your parent – swearing, smoking, drinking, noise, certain TV programs, etc.

❑ Set guidelines for personal space.

Topic #4: Shared Resources

❏ Talk about use of the family vehicle – how often can the parent expect to use it, and what are their responsibilities when they do?

❏ What about the family computer?

❏ Have the conversation about TV programs, and work out a way to deal with any scheduling conflicts between programs you and your parent want to watch.

Appendix 3:
Family Budget Template

Housing	Current Costs	Additional costs
Mortgage or rent		
Phone		
Electric		
Gas		
Water and sewer		
Cable		
Waste removal		
Maintenance or repairs		
Supplies		
Other		
Subtotals		

Transportation		
Car payment		
Insurance		
Licensing		
Fuel		
Maintenance		
Other		
Other		
Subtotals		

Percentage to be paid by parent	Parent's Share	Notes

Insurance	Current Costs	Additional costs
Home		
Health		
Life		
Other		
Subtotals		

Food

	Current Costs	Additional costs
Groceries		
Other		
Subtotals		

Pets

	Current Costs	Additional costs
Food		
Medical		
Grooming		
Toys		
Other		
Subtotals		

Percentage to be paid by parent	Parent's Share	Notes

www.ingramcontent.com/pod-product-compliance
Lightning Source LLC
Chambersburg PA
CBHW022135280326
41933CB00007B/706